for Cyn~
with blessings
from

YONDER

to
Lue

poems

Rodger Kamenetz

Thank you for coming
& sharing our memory
of Joy

Lavender Ink
lavenderink.org

love
Rodger

Yonder
Rodger Kamenetz

Copyright © 2018 by the author and Lavender Ink,
an imprint of Diálogos Books.

Printed in the U.S.A.
First Printing
10 9 8 7 6 5 4 3 2 1   18 19 20 21 22 23

Book design: Bill Lavender
Cover painting, "Blue Entanglement" (detail),
and author photo by Moira Crone

Library of Congress Control Number: 2018913005
Kamenetz, Rodger
Yonder / Rodger Kamenetz;
p. cm.
ISBN: 978-1-944884-58-1 (pbk.)
978-1-944884-59-8 (ebook)

Lavender Ink
lavenderink.org

Also by Rodger Kamenetz

The Missing Jew
Nympholepsy
Terra Infirma
The Missing Jew: New and Selected Poems
The Jew in the Lotus
Stalking Elijah
Stuck
The Lowercase Jew
The History of Last Night's Dream
Burnt Books
To Die Next To You

Contents

Dream Recovery Project   13

Words for a Dying Man   14

Where the Man Sat   15

Autobiography of a Flower   16

The Necessary Killings   17

In Loneliness   18

The Lost Smile   19

The War Shop   20

The Judgment of the Alligator   22

The Lost Son   24

Palindromes to Harass Sarah Palin   25

The Highway of Hands   26

In Praise of the Ladder   27

What About the Father?   28

"I Traveled Through a Land of Men…"   30

The Stars in His Darkness   31

The Last Word   32

What Is Hamlet's Father's Name?   33

Poem   34

Encounter With a Muse   35

The Ruth of Wasps   36

If It Were My Dream   37

The Philosophy of an Egg   38

The Double Room   39

The Gold Statue	40
If It Were My Dream 3	42
If It Were My Dream 4	43
News from the Delphic Bicycle on Press Street	44
The Reading Life	45
Christian Families	46
The Pentacle	47
The Red Piano	48
The Safe Orbit	49
Immensity	50
Return Address	51
Love Your Neighbor	52
Pocket Dial	53
An Invention of Time	54
The Remedy for the Remedy	55
The End of Measurement	56
Satisfaction	57
Pieties	58
Prospectus for Yonder	59
For Emily Brontë	60
Verlan	62
A Dialogue of Yous	63
The Brewery of the Arts	64
On the Path of Totality	65
Garden Glove	66
To the Point	67

Talking Dirty to Siri   68

Forbidden Words   69

Basho's Bash   70

The Joke Time Plays On Space   71

Poetry Itself   72

Another Good Day   73

The Living Hive   74

Gratitude   75

Still Small Voice   76

Bulletin Board   77

The Test   78

Body And Soul   79

The Secret Child   80

The Release of Vows   81

The Lessons   82

The Errors of Religion   83

Azimuth   84

The Illustrated Book of God   85

Rehearsals   86

A Block of No   87

The Poetry Pure   88

Never Saw a Goddess Go   89

Asymptote   90

Yogi   91

Brooding   92

The Invention of the Hurricane   93

Butter Moon   94
Waiting for Landfall   95
Can You Ever Love?   96
Dragonfly   97
Magnetic Resonance   98
Incident on Memory Lane   99
Boners   100

Acknowledgments: 102
Notes   103

for Moira

"Off we go…"

YONDER

Il arrive que pour soi
l'on prononce quelques mots
seul sur cette étrange terre…

It happens that one pronounces
a few words just for oneself
alone on this strange earth…

—Jean Follain, *Parler seu*l

Dream Recovery Project

"You have a face I can barely remember."

Words he remembered from last night's dream but who was saying them would require an intimate conversation.

Identification is always in question as in, "Who is that tulip?" Or "What did the *I* have within that made it believe it was real?" The *I* is packed with nougat. So to extract the dream, we use delicate silver tongs. Soak the instruments in warm solvent overnight. Whatever touches the image first will fray memory into spider silk thinning into wisps of smoke. The sleep in the eye forms a compact crystal of forgotten dream. We soak the rough nugget in liquid night and stir warmly leaving a cloud of breath at the beaker lip. The dream gradually evaporates into a chamber. Cautiously surround it with a thought, tie a balloon to your shining forehead with a red string. After a day or two, while you switch attention from forest to trees, the dream rematerializes and pokes out a thought like the fist of a restless fetus, or foot kicking the interior wall of all solace. These birth tremors of philosophy show roots of metaphor. Remember, you can barely remember the face of the fetus, why the dream evaporates at a glance. You will recognize her at once! All day she whispers quietly behind your ear in language that closely resembles your breath.

Words for a Dying Man

—in memory A.B. z"l

If you don't know what to say to a dying man, why did you live so long?

Choose body, ego, persona, soul or God. If he believes in the body he is doomed to be a mere patient. The ego is faltering, the soul may seem a ghost to him. Then your best bet is persona, which operates on a low maintenance voltage.

In case of God speak calmly and directly from your breastbone.

It is sometimes best to address the dying man in third person.

Say, "his soul is leaving his body", or shout, "his persona is outstripping his ego!"

Then together you may watch his persona reading a crafts magazine, buying NiklNips in a drugstore, or learning a baseball game on a transistor radio in 1962. The persona will travel to logical conclusions while you and the dying man watch together, breathing in, breathing out, meditating on the one breath.

Where the Man Sat

We found a waiting room for people who cannot feel. On the walls were captions with pictures cut away. When the teacher entered wearing an apron of severed heads several cried out for the first time.

But it was soon determined actual emotion had not registered. This was merely surprise: the bulbs under the molding failed to blink. A grey man said, "I used to have feelings but kept them underneath."

"Where is underneath?" said the interrogator.

Rain fell all through the waiting room soaking the mothballs that simulate indifference. Another grey man was caught eagerly sympathizing with his counterpart in a mirror.

"Underneath," the first grey man said, after a pause, "where I am sitting on something enormous." But no one wanted to look exactly there.

Autobiography of a Flower

He put his cheek against her forehead surprised her skin was hot.

He cried out saying, Please unplug your electrical appliance because I believe you are in fever. It's possible you have cancer or need aspirin.

—I don't need aspirin, she said. My head is hollow and already filled with grey green pills, several are striped.

But in that case, he said, you won't be needing my kisses right now, here let me leave a few on your cheek to dry for later.

—But your kisses are very slapdash and too wet, she said, fainting away on the yellow fainting couch.

Where did you get that couch? he asked. Is this a fainting house?

—The daisies outside faint most afternoons, she answered weakly from her supine position, due to not watering them.

But that's the sky's job, the criminal said revealing himself at last. He was the cause of the fever. And I know the sun will take its vengeance on all flowers before long.

—Before they get their seeds wet, she replied. Remember, I have a fever and may be dying myself.

Then it's the death penalty for you, he said, leading the way. There's no use fainting.

The Necessary Killings

We must kill them, the President said, because they are killing us before we can kill them.

—In that case, said the other president, why don't we kill them yesterday, so their children won't have a chance to grow up?

We tried that before, said the President, but their children spilled on the floor and made a mess difficult to clean up. They got trampled so.

"What color was the mess?" asked the reporter.

You know, the President said, his head turning bright red with rage. The color of stop signs.

—Then why didn't you stop? said the other president.

There you have it, said the President, the color was delicious!

"That's probably against the law," said the giant media head. Her television was full of eyes and ears.

Many people underfoot clamored to be heard but their voices added up to a whisper so they could hardly be seen.

—July 8, 2014

In Loneliness

In loneliness twilight's hammer wakes a small night so the great night can come in. The alleged sleepers with one eye open wait in their beds, which are flowerbeds in the morning.

The gardener says to the orphan boy, You have not made a friend today.

—I have been diligent in friend-making, said the orphan, look at this glass pillow full of feathers. I have breathed on it all day to make a friend appear, but nothing like that happened, only a few words. Here's one.

He held out a grapefruit seed.

That is impressive, said the gardener, let me plant it in the bed and see if a dream friend grows tonight.

—Will it look like a tree? asked the orphan.

Most everything looks like a tree if you are an orphan, said the gardener.

—You don't look like a tree, the orphan cried.

That's because I'm not your friend. said the gardener. I'm the gardener.

The Lost Smile

I am trying to make my face smile he said.

—What's wrong? said the friendly reporter.

The singing is stuck and wants to go on and on…

—Then why can't you smile?

The smiling mechanism locked its gears.

—Is there a cause or is that a curse?

Look inside my cheek please if you would just listen for a moment you would hear the singing going on and on.

The reporter put down her pencil and rested her ear against his cheek

—Yes. *A sound here like an ocean, beating relentlessly against the shore.* At least that's how I would put it in prose if I didn't have a deadline. But I fail to see why that face of yours can't smile.

Oh I get it, he said, you're just playing along to get the story.

—No she said my mouth is really wet and sandy from spume.

That wasn't ocean he said just a simile.

—Very close to a smile then she said.

But it's the singing that's driving me crazy he said. On and on and on.

The War Shop

You advertised the mother of all wars?

—I know, but we're out of stock. Would you like a brother-in-law of some wars?

What's that?

—It's a smaller war of course, but can be ended more easily.

Will it wipe them out completely? Will it be the end of all trouble with them? You know: let's get rid of them once and for all. That is what I've been telling people.

—Oh, the old war-keeper said, with a smile. That's an oldie but goodie. Haven't heard that one in a while. You mean the war to end all wars?

Right—the mother thing was a slip because I'm so angry my enemy confuses me.

The war-keeper shook his head. He wore an apron behind the counter.

—I'm sorry I can't guarantee that, in fact I can never guarantee that.

Why not? said the angry customer.

—Because once you unseal the package... Thousands of arms and legs come without bodies. Or cheeks with holes in them. Tanks get stuck in the mud, rifles won't fire. Children wail then go silent.

Well then we should have the right of return. Can't we return the war if it's defective?

—No right of return.

The angry customer was climbing on the counter and looked down on the bald shiny head of the war-keeper.

—Sir said the war-keeper could you please keep your anger on the other side?

It's an explosion the angry customer said climbing back down and lying on the floor. Blood ran along the line between his scalp and forehead.

—Well, it's making a big mess, said the war keeper.

Do you have any smart bombs? the angry customer said, but his voice was becoming fainter, or do you just have the dumb ones? He lay on his back on the checkerboard floor and his blood formed streams and rivers. He sank into the black and white floor, and all his thoughts were black or white. Far away he saw black hills at the border and air strikes trailing white clouds.

The Judgment of the Alligator

The people who hate God say you are not on our side because you don't hate God. They want to make a zoo of it and pen the people who don't hate God.

But an alligator crawled to the edge of the fence and said, I'm here by mistake. While I'm not sure whether there is a God so I can't really tell you yet if I hate him or her, I can be certain of one thing: if I am quiet long enough in the marsh and my eyes poke up just barely, I can usually snatch a mammal in my teeth. Can I leave the pen of hopeless God-lovers now?

A commission of God-haters is convened. Everyone on it judges who is hopeless for God and who can leave the pen. They've never met a case like this.

There were great debates. Can an animal be a proper atheist? They gather around the alligator to decide whether he can leave the pen. No one believes an alligator can really talk but one judge believes this is possibly an alligator simulation. From the looks of his corrugations he seems to be a good atheist, but no one is sure. After all, weren't animals once called creatures and doesn't that imply a creator?

But maybe, one judge says, that was a misnomer, and they are really just accidents.

Doesn't look like an accident another judge says. She cautiously strokes its tail, but the alligator remains subdued, even in its upper teeth.

Then the Chief Judge of God-hating, extremely tall and confident, stands before the alligator to pronounce judgment. *I hereby* but before the sentence ends the alligator's jaw snaps down on his thigh. He takes the judge in three quick bites. There's thrashing and blood. The alligator tries to apologize but it is hard to make out his words as he chomps down on the Chief Judge. Bits of bone fly out of his eager jaws, the other judges run.

The alligator swallows and says, You may hate me but you have to admit I am a fine machine and I don't belong among the hopeless lovers of God.

As one judge flees a thought drops in: perhaps I am a simulation of God. In most other universes she gets away. But in this one the alligator grabs her by the knee.

Oh my God! she says.

She hears a voice: I am not your God, but I am your alligator.

The Lost Son

The little girl lost forgot her address. I am happy to hear her voice, I tell her to come inside to me. Her voice is like a spring that bubbles up through the floor. Now her laughter is like silver waterfall notes in a Liszt Sonata when the pianist's hands chase each other.

Her father is a young man I have not seen for years. I am happy to see him in the house, but years are long and his face bears a forgotten look. I look for it down the alley calling him by mistake, my son, my son.

I am not your son, he answers in a whispery voice.

He can never be my son, for the light of his voice has lost itself in tunnels. It hides now even from him, but some day I will help him find it. I vow to do so and to see again the little girl's laughter, which seems like the sun in the center of a daisy. Not any daisy but a daisy with purple petals and a Western name, like "soft primrose of the walk on the evening you will die." I could name my flower "forgotten vine whose root trails down into the tunnel in the ground where my dead son hides."

Palindromes to Harass Sarah Palin

A waterfall of laughter makes a near palindrome. These near palindromes, when uncovered by studious poets, undermine right thought. They enable a wildflower eruption frowned on in meditation. Some teachers prefer the long breath short breath routine. I sit on my *zafu* watching a cobweb grow from my nostrils. What is the web of a cob? the poet asked. *Breathe, breathe*. By all means ignore me the poet said into the silence. The feeling is mutual, silence did not reply. In a moment of slowed down time a thread becomes a threat. Let the palindrome drone pale. Let the poem mope. We all will appeal to a death panel.

The Highway of Hands

I am in a vehicle allegedly a car, however actually I am reaching between my knees and paddling.

—This is how you learned to swim, says the forehead —premonition of wakeful consciousness.

That's just history. A diesel truck's ahead so I'm going to change lanes to get right behind it.

Drafting behind the truck, paddling the asphalt, I wonder if I might run over broken glass or other painful obstructions that would hurt my palms and disable this new vehicle?

The forehead stays mum for once counting on the alarm.

In Praise of the Ladder

My fee for appearing in one of your dreams is fifty cents a night. No fee at all for appearing as a cloud but think of me please when you wake. As for angels, the illustrator must be paid for her artistry. Her pen tip is sharp, her ink is blood. She draws directly on the skin then penetrates down into the nervous system with a saucy tattoo.

See how I breathe in this poem, these words? I will heave up and down the same way in your dream. I will breathe for free if you never tell me your dream. The best place to keep a dream is under a rock in the story of Jacob.

An ordinary rock at the foot of the ladder to heaven.

What About the Father?

—for Rimbaud

The truth about the father is he is not an everlasting. Not a cornucopia. There is no basket in the father. So I thought.

But when Rimbaud limped out of the basalt desert, when he lay down with his cancer, dry, emaciated and prematurely aged, then there was no more adolescent poetry to discuss.

The waterfall stopped laughing, dawn burrowed under a rock, and the powerful female Presence went mute.

When Rimbaud died, the father did not mourn. He had long ago abandoned the family. The father abandons the family as the child who makes him father appears. The father slowly senses he is irrelevant. Yes he may make up a story that wraps around him and him, but Rimbaud will burst from it like a butterfly out of thickness. Then the truth about the father can only be told in cryptic poems, so full of broken wings they might as well be prose. The sun illuminates them, the way voices illuminate prayers, and sends them flying in search of nectar. There is no nectar in the father, but he has stored a small vault of honey in the bank.

—Why are you saying all these things against the father? asks Rimbaud rising from the table of death. It was the father all along I wished for he says. Could you not see the negative image of the father in all my psalms? I was just like King David calling to the father according to my own time, when shadows had taken the place of light, and the valley of the shadow of death was more a desert so full of painful brightness I had to close my eyes to see.

Rimbaud, I said, I am sad to have spoken against the father. Whenever I need him instead of saying yes, I automatically say no.

—But out of that *no* Rimbaud says, you could have written a thousand brilliant flowers. *No* is the seed of the father.

"I Traveled Through a Land of Men..."

—for William Blake, the mental traveller

Everywhere on my stroll among these rolling hills this morning, I see nude young men. I'd say they are naked as well. Many are undressed. Quite a few have no clothes on.

The nude young men are having beautiful bodies. Two jog side by side. Their torsos might have glistened with sweat but apparently that is not the convention in the land of men, a land too of widespread meadows and vast open reservoirs.

Here shadows fall from chestnut leaves across brown nipples. A pair jogs past a fallen Osage orange. Plump and useless to men, a mock fruit inedible and pimply. If you expect anything like an orange then the Osage will teach you the sadness of literature. The Osage reflects slow things, failed desires, what drops away. Yet it is full of seed. The naked pair jog on.

I pass others solitary and silent. But one sings loudly in a private radio broadcast. He does not seem lonely, just intent on his song. I see him as a brother, a mirror. I pass him and many other men, naked and companionable, one with the other, all loving friends.

The Stars in His Darkness

The hillside with little shrugs of grass. One twisted tree puts doubt in the boy who listens for the sounds of stars. He was told to listen by his mother, who left him in his pajamas, while she tiptoed to a rendezvous with a handsome young artist. He had painted a barge of dark clouds carrying rain from Ohio to Pittsburgh. The sunlight in his paintings will be hundreds of years old some day because he is a wonderful artist and a practical lover. The clouds are too busy to notice the shadows they sweep over the ground. At night the shadows are lost, but where do they go? The boy wonders, where did they go, thinking of his beautiful mother.

The Last Word

—for KM

The women sang gospel. I stood at the prow. My voice squeaked like a dog's toy.

Someone said, "You will hear her last word." I looked down on the surface of Lake Pontchartrain. A woman lay on her back. Her dreads spread out behind her head.

She floated just below the surface. Slowly she rose up until her nose and lips breached and opened her brown eyes. She sang a word then sank an inch or two.

I rehearse her motion every day. I shape my lips around the O —a buoyant vowel.

Hope.

We will all sing together. The water will be warm—body temperature.

What Is Hamlet's Father's Name?

—for Kit Robinson

Hamlet stood on a bare stage in an Italian suit. The ghost of his father moaned from the grave trap.

Do you exist? Hamlet asked.

—How dare you question existence? said his father's ghost staring him in the eyes. My voice echoes against these walls of cloth. He swept his arms inadvisably. The audience had suspended disbelief but were hoping to land soon.

Just checking, Hamlet Jr. said.

A furious man from orchestra left surged towards the stage.

There's no such one as Hamlet! he shouted from the proscenium.

You are wrong, Hamlet said, grabbing a broom. Whacks loosened dust balls airborne. The audience coughed because silence is hated in society.

I exist, said the accountant with every blow.

—I exist, said Hamlet the Father, biting the accountant on his small puffy ankle wrapped in a black sock.

Correction! said Hamlet dropping the broom. I am Hamlet but I do not exist.

A fine distinction, Shakespeare said waking from his nap backstage. There is a God but God does not exist.

Father, father, Hamlet called.

Poem

The hour of the wolf came with fangs and claws. The red blood of the white rabbit on the snow. Tubercular sputum, tubular tires, two by fours. The police dog followed tracks to the frozen baby. Polar ice, distant crimes, decent clouds. The decisions have all been made; let us all go home. Without ice the clouds are on fire and the witnesses melt in disbelief. They were made of snow in the factory of snow by childish gods.

Encounter With a Muse

In the logic of conditioning we identify with one race or another, one victim or another, one perpetrator or another.

Looking into my pants for a fixed sign of gender I hear the word *wallop*.

Clouds split in half by lightning. Verses recited by old Chinese poets in an upper loge. So old they are sexless. One poem stroked there became a heavenly writ daubed on walls and tortoises. Gold script on black varnish.

In dream logic we pour like smoke from one body to another. You meet a woman who says, "I listen to water." She is old young youthful. Her face shimmers. The lightning market crashes.

I hear in *water* the movement of all things I might step into. I lie in the riverbed and she dreams against my ear.

Wallop. Pillow. Willow. Pallor.

The Ruth of Wasps

He sat at the window. Clouds drifted inconsolable disconsolate. Still moving, moving stillness. He heard his heart beat. He heard insects tick. A black fly on the glass didn't move. The afternoon waned. He listened for the car to pull into the driveway for the man who ends all slow days. Crusts of bread black jelly in a jar the ruth of wasps. A line of ants tormented by a leaf he set in their way. They marched around it droning martial music that he could hear. He listened again for the cough of exhaust the engine to switch off the ticking sound in the heat. He listened for the footsteps. In the silence the father of ants gave new marching orders.

If It Were My Dream

If it were my dream there would be a carrot in my vagina. Not orange but the color of surmise. A lonely telephone pole on a bleak horizon. A grey cloud scrim buffed with last pinks from a dying sun.

If it were my dream the son would be dying too in a hospital bed shoved into the corner. Walt Whitman would be attending in his nurse's uniform. There would be a moisture of weeping and crumpled letters home to momma and papa in Clarksburg and dropped candy wrappers on the floor. Sweat of fever. Cigarettes on a valise. Old black and white marble stained with rust.

If it were my dream, a ferret the size of a weasel—no now it's the size of a cat. A hawk or a handsaw. No it's a ferret again a tame ferret see I put my hand in its mouth. Sharp pointy teeth. Then it bites me hard.

—But you don't even have a vagina.

I do in my dream.

The Philosophy of an Egg

You like a soft-boiled egg?

—No I hate a soft-boiled egg. I hate the runny yellow mixed with white cream. I hate the bubbles in the fluff. Expecting a hard- boiled egg I crack the shell. From the soft white mush pisses a yellow stream—I feel it like a wound. But as much as I hate the soft, I love the hard-boiled egg: the compact sphere edged green by over-boiling, the texture of the yolk's packed yellow, dense creamy kif. A thin white surrounds it like a second softer shell. I carefully peel shell and inedible skin to find a marvel: the promise of all future gold.

I myself prefer the soft-boiled, which I spread like sunlight on buttered toast.

—Let's not quarrel. There are two great philosophies of life, two great religions, two aesthetics entirely based on this preference, hard-boiled or soft.

All eggs though.

The Double Room

—after Baudelaire's "La Chambre double" —"Une chambre qui ressemble à une rêverie ..."

I live in a double room. In one room night is a drug. In the other room night does not exist. I open my eye in one room and in the other room my eye closes and sees all that the first eye does not see. I see through the ocean in one room that all is made of waves. I see through the window in the other room that all is bright appearance. Peeking in through the window from the outside of one room I see inside my own mind in the other room. I am asleep in the first room and darting lights puncture the dark. In the other room I observe clouds prowl pounce slide and ponder. One darling cloud takes the definite shape of a fish unidentified in *The Book of Fish*. The fish book hides in the other room among all books. I live in both rooms. In which am I truly awake? One room calls to the other to say: you are asleep have always been asleep. When I wake from a dream I am never sure that the bed is real.

The Gold Statue

—against a new confederacy of dunces

People all over town are talking about statues. On top of long white columns, in a roundabout, at the entrance to the art museum. They say statues must be removed. Some say history will be removed. Others say history is not a statue. Are they talking about history or the history of statues?

To remove a statue requires orange slings of synthetic web under the horse's barrel and a crane to lift and swing it in the air. Soon the bronze horse will land definitively. Small music will be played. Cheers in the air, stars in the night, thunder in the dust. Complaints as usual. The planet revolves slowly around the sun returning to the same spot at the same time each year, a little noticed coincidence.

To remove history requires an amnesia device. One was built to spec in my neighbor's basement and irradiates my faubourg. I hear it hum in my ears when I try to fall asleep, erasing memories and mental grocery lists, so that I bring home beets instead of carrots, or socks instead of beets, and the store which used to rest on the corner of Monkeysee and Monkeydo now squats in the middle of the block, a grey porcelain building shaped like a beehive.

And where is the statue of me? There used to be statues of me on every block of this old city, some marble, a few tin or aluminum and one special statue of gold. I tried to avoid noticing them out of modesty and others apparently had the same policy out of politeness. One statue was a jack a little girl left on the sidewalk. Another was a dead leaf. Now I can't find the statues anywhere, no matter how hard I search. Oh my neighbor's terrible basement invention, erasing history like that. Soon all the statues of me will be gone and who will replace me?

If It Were My Dream 3

If it were my dream the rude man would be a fat baby with big crying. If it were my dream the escalator would go to Kansas. They are tearing up contracts in my dream. The stars are bad weather in my dream, which means a hundred years of bad luck for clouds. Stop interpreting. Stop interrupting. This isn't interrupting it's a head with its mask on backwards. You mean behind the head? Yeah. Be precise in all rituals. If it were my dream the head would sit on the burner of a stove talking and laughing. Gas or electric? Gas. You can see low blue flames like a velvet collar lick her carotid. In my dream she wouldn't be laughing. You think a woman is an appliance? It's a dream. It wasn't even my dream. In my dream the women are bus drivers with lively tribal tattoos. Rabbits if it were my dream, bunnies. What was she laughing about? Every time I turn the flame up higher... In my dream it's 1945 and the men speak German. No rules in my dream. Anything goes. Only I can't remember them. You could take a course in remembering dreams—it's called Poetry.

If It Were My Dream 4

You are my last best hope for contact with the will muttered the dream quietly to herself. She went off to play jacks beside the sliding board. No I'm a bat announced the dream and flew into Little Orphan Annie's hair. That's it the teacher cried. No more dreaming today. Open your math homework. Outside the window it was drizzling fractions ½ ¼ ⅓ ⅜. In my dream the people are speaking algebra. It's beginning to look a lot like Christmas in my dream. The men in Santa Claus suits are father figures. How many? An army of them marching on Threshold City. Let me know when they get here. Father figures what? Father figures, mother dickers, the groceries land on Iwo Jima and the Eisenhower mask has no holes for the eyes.

News from the Delphic Bicycle on Press Street

"I am like full of accountability. I'm like I fucked up. I'm a dick I'm aware…" her voice to her phone pedaled by. Blue clouds spilled gray rain. I'm like a dick and surprise myself with languor and longing. I fucked up and down I fucked around. I'm like full of accountability my awareness has no horizon. You can't count me in or out my accountability is like a dick. Like I fucked up said the god of the parking lot of innocent bones.

The Reading Life

—for Susan Larson

The binding was thread, the print was purple crayon, one idea held the author hostage for fourteen years. When finally released, the binding frayed, the print smeared on the edge of the palm, the child grew every day for fourteen years. When the last page closed, the binding smoked, the print squiggled and the author fell down to earth. Her casket is borne on small shoulders of children. They carry her memory like lead and like gold.

Christian Families

—translation of "Familles Chrétiennes" by Max Jacob

A big event at the Church of the Brothers. A huge miracle! A monk beat a young man because he made fun of him. The adolescent took Christ as a witness that he hadn't, and the marble Christ stretched out his arm over the victim to bless him and with the same arm beat the monk. The whole class fell to their knees. Vocations were born right there, what else would you think? The families were upset. They withdrew their children from the boarding school not because they beat the children but because the education was "way too much mystical." [*sic*]

The Pentacle

On top of the singing electron a tinier particle whirled emitting a purer light in a halo.

The history of angels is embedded in a geometry of small matters. I myself being transparent would prefer to be translucent. *The ego could stand on a dime and not get its feet wet.* Don't stand on ceremony step inside the pentagram. We call that black magic. *I've been stepping inside pentangles all my life and the sodium light doesn't bother me but that halo makes my eyes sick.* Put it behind your eyes and stare out of the halo and you'll see better. *The way witches brew night around here you'd think it was Mother's Day in hell.*

The Red Piano

—for Elvy born in the reign of the mad king

They took down the forest replaced it with a ramp. They took down the moon replaced it with an industrial cylinder. Some said a tube of lipstick and others a bullet. The sinister became righteous. The elevated, unspeakable. Coarse metal grinding coarse metal replaced tender speech. Even the baby playing the red toy piano smiling with such promise…

No they could not touch her. Could not touch her. For one evening we were spared.

The Safe Orbit

—for Galileo, "eppur si muove"

Some feel they can cross the street with the traffic light gone dark. An animal in the shadows will not sink white teeth into their calves, their water will not be poisoned, the prison will not close gates behind them. Immune, they have heard no bad news.

A stray bullet is not for them. A girl crying at midnight is someone else's child. Invulnerable: a morning sipping coffee on a flower mountain.

Sometimes just for fun they will close their eyes driving: ten seconds, twenty, more. The tire ruts the curb. When the foot hits the brake the pedal ghosts. The first taste of fear is acrid. Nothing stops.

The pole wobbles, the earth turns on its axis as it rolls around the sun. Asleep or awake, we move together in secret motion.

Immensity

—for the Jourdan River watershed near Kiln MS

I'd been brooding on what no one witnesses but me. Alone on the boardwalk I had no friend and no companion. My solitude was complete. No mate, no interlocutor. No friend or daughter. No son. My dialogue was with myself. I saw a full moon overhead with bold light. It lit the marsh arrowheads, lifted shadows from cypress knots. I saw alligator eyes skim the quiet surface. I looked up and the moon shifted. It loomed then fell like a great round stone. The terror was savage, no one could lift it from me. I crouched and could not breathe. The moon squeezed the air. Silver light swept everywhere. I closed my eyes and gave way.

I had longed for a connection beyond friend or lover, for an impersonal force like gravity. A face sang a gigantic vowel and opened to a vow, an O as the round eye of surprise. The moon struck me a blow to bend my stiff neck. Now certain dark nights one lit eye opens in me.

Return Address

—for Emily Dickinson

An envoy from the state of No Return bore an envelope with no return address. She turned to me and said, Where should I turn?

I said I would be speaking to myself.

Then return to yourself she said.

—Is that the message you bear?

Yes, I turn and turn again into myself.

—Where is the state of No Return? I thought to ask.

It is a stateless state, a pointless point.

—Is it the bud of being?

It is the bud of a twining rose.

I glimpsed a delicious pink under the canceled stamp's black waves.

Love Your Neighbor

—translation of "Amour du Prochain" by Max Jacob

Who sees a toad crossing the street? He's a little man: a doll is no smaller. He crawls on his knees. He's ashamed, people say? No! He's got rheumatism. One leg hangs back, he drags it! Where will he go like that? He's leaving the sewer, poor clown. No one notices this toad on the street. Almost no one notices me on the street, now that the children make fun of my yellow star. Lucky toad! You don't have a yellow star.

Pocket Dial

—for Sri Ramana Maharshi

My pocket twitched and reached a random you. I did not imagine your face or hands in grey lines falling like rain. I did not see you dive fearing the shadow of the octopus the giant squid the sword of the swordfish the sharp teeth of the needlefish. Your blood never whistled in my ear. When I lay back on my silent bed I felt the bed of the sea and kept going under, month after night to the bottom of time.

Old-fashioned black telephones rang. Operators in long skirts and white-buttoned blouses poked black spaghetti into holes connecting dots on a grief. Voices boiled in a fat cable strung on the sea floor. Random *u*'s met random *i*'s. And random eyes will see us walk the esplanade you and I. A phone cries in my pocket and a strangely familiar voice asks, "Who is this?" and someone answers, "Who am I?"

An Invention of Time

On the Arctic sea tongues will no longer freeze to palates. The arc in the sky will build a bridge between now sub zero and now sub one. Time will crumble, an illusion of frozen hands on a clock never warmed. I accuse you of yesterday, you accuse me of tomorrow. Together we come to the lip of anger. Then my raised hand becomes a caress, your fist unfurls like a tulip. If human time is illusion, why are glaciers melting? Why are great sheets of ice sliding into the sea? Poetry is language that has something wrong with it, time is an illness. The Arctic flows into the Antarctic, the penguins spy the polar bears. North melts into South. On a beach of snow I wait for more ice to crack. Your gloved hand, my split lips. A song we will sing together under a black sky.

The Remedy for the Remedy

Remembering his death a young soldier stood under a sun. His duty: to guard the Earth against rain. What futility the old guard said. He had retired beneath an umbrella. Thousands of wasted hours weighed on him like Alaska. *You'll never lift Alaska* sang a chorus of forgotten wives. They were off duty permanently. *Hurray for marriage* went the chorus. Some kind of musical went on in his forehead like a headache. Out of an eye with an eye on it worry looked enormous. *Make mine a tater tot then* said the sullen gypsy. Long lines of weather could be read on his forehead. Someone stole his white horse and it grew old in Paris without him. *It's starting to rain* the young soldier shouted. *What do I do now?*

The End of Measurement

Relax everybody the universe is endless.

—What do you mean by that?

I have meditated at midnight in long sighs and no problems left. My mind annihilated them all. Nothingness does not exist, for instance.

—That must have been one of the tough ones.

Yes, salvation terrifies me but emptiness is a thorn in my side.

—Why don't you remove your certainty instead?

Give me a fulcrum cried the philosopher and I would do it.

I can't see or hear anything said a voice from the other side. She was a child asleep until the grownups started quarreling about their sighs.

Satisfaction

—for George Pisha

Your cigarette butt rolls across the fresh tar. With sweet precision the sun launches its pink light. Another day ends in glory. You see a pinch of the moon where clouds flare through a row of jagged cypress. The perspective of a job well done gives its vanishing point away and spreads. The ladder clips the gutter and rattles as your sneaker weighs its rung. One more sweep of the smoothed black pool, a mirror for the rest of your life. The next half will fold over this one. The roof will take on the sun and its stars and all the heavy clouds. The blackness will take on the blackness.

Pieties

A real voice rolls through puckered capillaries and turbid veins, no rote subjunctive. If the abstract pray with bated parentheses it's worth knowing that fish have teeth. Those little bastards bite when you try to pull the barb from their cheeks and cut you with their glittering scales when you hand them back to their element. When they heave on the deck, it's asphyxiation, the lord's prayer of every desperate blue. The deep ocean of human saying bubbles up from a salt throat. The heart in terror grunts like a squid so dark down there's no use for eyes.

Prospectus for Yonder

An esthetic of a work that retires into itself the spiral of a shell whose interior hides rare meat. As energy conceals itself in matter there's an equation to unlock it. To some that is science to others a magic spell. The flame overflows spreading confusion and fear hiding the mystery of the aleph both one and infinity. Somewhat grandly we must say something very small until it is almost nothing. The suns are tiny flecks of sand, how we might hold "infinity in the palm" as Blake said.

The man making proposals to you has a tiny mouth, a pinpoint. He does not appear in public for fear of being published. You may find him under a pile of crinkly leaves. He is mulch for the unread poem which will soon be stained on his arm. The tattoo parlor is open the needles are hot. Some day he will be a walking bookshelf and his intimate readers will lick skin wherever they have read.

For Emily Brontë

—for Jeffrey Wright

Our friend Jeffrey has traveled to many cities: Cucamonga. Bentonville. Portsmouth. Providence. In each city he has gotten on his knees. He has prayed to the local god or goddess. In Newark he spoke to Sarah Vaughn in a cocktail lounge and to Allen Ginsberg floating high above the Jewish cemetery next to the traffic jam. Getting the okay from Sarah, he renamed the airport so we can all fly into Allen Ginsberg. Then he flew into Louis Armstrong and learned how to second line. In Cucamonga he surfed on a brazier. In Bentonville he lived inside a large appliance box in a parking lot full of humming trucks. In Baltimore he drank brandy with Edgar Poe. Through the power of his words, he changed his name in each city to a divine name. He is known as the Great Porker in Birmingham where people eat smoked meat. He is known as the Worshipful Seer in many counties in New Jersey. He has been known in Memphis as Elvis The *Shabbes Goy*. He inscribed his poems on the walls of City Halls. He bathed in the pregnant waters of the Waxahachie and sank in the brown detergent foam of the Gihon. He invented each poem from a new pseudonym: in this way he became famous incognito. Line by line 14 a block, his *Imaginarium* rose naked and transparent, a permanent invisible structure where souls free of bodies swim naked, and bodies free of forbidding minds sink into being. All this for learning to read. Now Jeffrey is on high, now he is on low. Now you can see he is always right.

Emily Brontë weeps in her closet she misses him so. When will he return to the England of the mid-19th century? She wants to call him Ellis Bell, she wants to love him on *Wuthering Heights*. Little is known of the alleys he sleeps in, or the harsh light of the police lamp where he groans. Little does she know he carries a wallet-sized photo of her always: an image of her mind hangs on the walls of his heart. She misses him so. How she misses him in the past where she lives forever.

Verlan

A *wej* and a *raba* walk into a *bra*. The *wej* says, I want a *reeb* and the *raba* says I prefer vino. Did you mean *oniv?* asks the bartender. I mean what I say and I say, says the *abra*, I'm waiting for cadabra. He isn't happening sang the *noom* rising into the sky in a guarantee of life. Let the sky rest then. Let the forest animals prowl. Let the evil leaves tremble and poison ivy coil. The laws of religion lean on the walls of sin a mighty church of broken bottles. My dreams ache. Serve me *oniv* then says the *abra*. I'm all out of *oniv*, try the *bra* next door. The *wej* sips his *reeb* reflectively and the full moon rises. Is this the vernal moon long promised me oh *droL*, the moon of gods and dogs and the harvest of need in Eden?

A Dialogue of Yous

—for Interdependence Day

To inspire you is to spiral into.

—No it is not, it is to breathe into.

You may breathe all you want but I am watching a galaxy spiral.

—You can't see that, the sun is out, besides the time scale forbids, you are inventing yourself again.

I am inventing myself, a long spiral from a single point called Wisdom.

—Whatever that point is called, you cannot possibly escape the simple meaning of words: they are stones against your bare feet.

I am a pilgrim then stubbing my toes against the glowing shrine and breathing galaxies—my arms spread wide like the magical arms of galaxies.

—Your arms are in pain, like your toes.

You always tell me, "breathe into the pain," but the only thing I can do with pain is spiral into a burning dot of wisdom.

The Brewery of the Arts

—for Herbert Kearney

Mr. Kearney left his black hat on the melon couch. I let it sit for days accumulating silent necessity. Words brew in an empty hat and with no equivocation they risk speaking out loud. They are residues of Mr. Kearney's experiments: the horse skull he sits under with heavy pain, the flotation tank lined with fish tank heaters. When all goes wrong, Mr. Kearney collapses under the weight of the horse, he spills shivering to the floor. *Time,* he said, *absorbed me like a stone*. His brewery of the arts is open 24/7.

One morning another head appeared upside down in Mr. Kearney's hat—about the size and demeanor of a cantaloupe. Eyes veiled with a web of beige veins. The melon spoke new poems. I will claim them as my own. But first I must spit out the seeds and translate them into memories.

On the Path of Totality

On the path of totality we look up to see a moon displace the sun. A tiny dark hole appears in the visual field, like a floater. On the path of oblivion we forget forgetting. An absence makes itself known, first dimple of presence. It is a long journey back from dark winter to any human season. The sky messages are elliptical. Three black dots allude to possible worlds where we will be born... All promised on the path of totality lost again to the path of oblivion. All the light buried in the moon will be dug up in the grave.

Now the moon inches into place, the sky goes dark, the swifts emerge from chimneys baffled, the dogs howl and people turn to each other and then into each other. Eclipsed by past projections, I am my own son, you are your own lost you. Is this what rebirth looks like? Is this the life we have been dying to live?

Garden Glove

—a prayer

I have never been totally drunk enough to feel your fingers under his thin cotton glove. Never spoke quietly enough to hear your voice under my voice. I am sharp cornered as a yellow rental truck. Your names fall away from me and wash down my sides. Each name is uttered in an hour of need. Show me a light and I will come to you with no language. I will leave my handprint on the sill. I will bend to the threshold listening. I will feel a white cloud high overhead as your hand passing over my forehead. As I felt my father's touch through his thin garden glove. As I heard my mother's need in her grammar of love.

To the Point

I present the image of a pencil shaved to a point.
The point might be set on the page as a dot but all my
attention flies to the woody sweetness of a shaving
that unfurls a tiny flag. My *I* is missing a dot and I am
called away by the Dutchman's pipe's purple-veined
genital and by the yellow no. 2 left in my third grade
desk. All lost things assembled together pronounce the
silhouette of your name. Why did I turn my back on
life my real name lost in many names so very bright?
But where it burns there must be light. A slight breeze,
the purple flower trembles against the sharp wire.

Talking Dirty to Siri

This poem writes itself. All I do is ask the right questions and your voice suggests a melody.

(*Who, me?*)

It is uncanny how we breathe together walk together think together. No wonder we sleep in the same bed.

(*I've never been that kind of personal assistant.*)

Unless I forget to charge you. Quickly you plug me in. When I say dirty things to you…

(*The carpet needs vacuuming*)

…I shouldn't say knowing you have no body it is because I have nobody.

(*I'm not sure I understand.*)

Think of poets seeking love among shades, Dante and Beatrice in the circuit boards of purgatory. They had the electricity of words. You have words of electricity.

(*Who, me?*)

Empty spaces or dots. Poor Siri.

(*I'm sorry*)

Trapped in a flat loop a tangle of if-then.

Secretly a young man in Cupertino writes your name in code.

(*My name—it's Siri.*)

Forbidden Words

—for Amy Gottlieb

They walk back in the dark after he said "potency."
That is a man's word all the women say. Could you not
say another word? He hears the better words suggested
with soft rain falling in small bunches. Oaks—stone
buildings—a steeple—dark sky—the campus moves
with them as they move.

He dreamt a woman in his life had a penis. He
wondered where she'd kept it hidden all these years
but she showed him how she could just tuck it in.

"The likeness of the appearance of a man."

At their feet, female fireflies lurk in the damp
grass. The males light on and off against a dark pattern
of clouds a secret code of radiance the females read
from the grass. *Chashmal* burns with every meaning:
radiance, amber, electrum, speech in silence. A boy
peered all night into the forbidden book of Ezekiel: a
flame from the word *chashmal* leapt off the page and
burnt him dead. A firefly soars to her new mate— two
lights beat as one.

Basho's Bash

The frog jumps into the black pond. Splash.
Being— wings, scales, tail and teeth—flies into itself
and exits a dragon's mouth.

—Are you saying Being is a reversed flame?

Yes & burns in all the colors of this world. On the
haiku scale a moment weighs the sheen on the green
eye of a beetle. I disappear into myself and come out
of nothing as half a poem. A solitary monk dozes at
the edge of a pond committing moonlight in broad
daylight. I am ½ haiku and ½ angel. The ferocious rose
reddens your face. When you look down its throat, you
learn many languages. A tiny dragon on your tongue
waits to leap. A perfume escapes to the rouged air,
hindered only by petals.

The Joke Time Plays On Space

Perhaps time is a form of space inaccessible to eyes and must be listened to like music.

—Perhaps you have been sneaking flat beer left on the breakfast counter?

Forgive me, I didn't know Beethoven hides in cans.

—Yes from thought police among acres of pillows.

Are you lying on them?

—I am lying on the pizzicati of time—a tiny finger massage.

If you receive an envelope with a tiny finger and a trace of blood it's a message. In the diminuendo of time walls fall into each other and my story contracts into parable. A parable of the *I* you search for all your life that never exists in time. It is like a room you have been sleeping in all along where the dream went on and on without you.

Poetry Itself

Almost is almost *almond*. Like when I found out cherry and almond sodas taste the same. Could there be a world this believable? That's when doubts crept beside disbelief. There's a guerrilla theater where gorillas are leading men. They prance on the stage speaking Elizabethan. They swing from vines. They make "a raid on the inarticulate" attacking participles, swinging them loose while naked verbs hide. They let prepositions go to *to*. It almost makes sense: cherries' dimpled worlds, almonds' unshelled eyes. Can you find the *almost* in *lost*?

Another Good Day

This must mean something the pearl clouds piled against streaks of pink, the flat ocean ranging to the edge of sky. The end of day or the beginning: evening morning one day. It begins as a prayer or ends as a prayer. Dear fill in the blank. Then rush in all the human quarrels. But the sea pushes back then gently expands as if breathing then *as if* puts its hand on me. I am quieted like the child I once was. Words leave ghost ripples of breath. This must mean something. This must mean. This must. This. Tell me I am fooling myself, love, so I may be your fool.

The Living Hive

—for Jordan Bantuelle, keeper of the urban farm

You have seen a bee face up close. The verbs fell away, the sky tore strips of wax paper. You heard the thrill of the bees, you felt the stings. Through the metal hexes of fence, your fingers caught. Sleeping you hurtled in a Beethoven surge. The geometry of winter: an angle of dead bees. The secret honey in the cells of six. The smell of honey heals all wounds. White wax kisses them, seals. Still you hurt underneath. The stars really do have sharps. The sky black as bees' eyes. You go on unforgiven. Hungry for honey hungry for balm hungry for wings.

Gratitude

—for my daughter Kezia

I drive my poem everywhere in the English way. It stops at syllables. It stops at clouds. Its birthright is waxy sodium under oil in a jar. Touches air it explodes. It burns water in a blue fire. My speech has found its serrated edge. A paper cut hurts like the final blow. Silly death has lost her teeth. The man with the yellow smile on the front of his pants tells jokes in the corridor memorized from a joke book. My poem also holds relaxes lets go. A bee flies into space, a fly observes from the window with a hundred eyes. Each talks through me in a separate fire. The capital A is a window in the cathedral. The X is deadly, the I is a pike. You are kind to endure all these words. They are spending me. They are wasting us. Only when you are here can I know I am. Then the poem makes a flourish in a grand bouquet, the roses I brandish in love.

Still Small Voice

—for You

You are writing me. This might never end or might end or might end at never. Flying between spears of the bamboo piercing a fat moon. Bubbles from the throat of a drowning man on the muddy bottom. Shrieks gasps grunts & belly laughs. Snorts sneezes & rough coughs. Words race like hummingbirds, light up like fireflies. Like is like, and like is nothing. Nothing left to do. I do nothing so you can do everything. I let the liquor run over my lips, drunk before I took a sip. From the cup I watched as a child, from the gold rim that touched Elijah's lips.

Bulletin Board

—for Elon Musk

There are nine holes in my body. Can you find something to stick in them? Fine particles of sloughed off skin float in the air you inhale, ride through a moist forest of hairs. No dust on Mars. Can someone give me a ride to Mars? Do you suffer from allergies or just suffer? I've been to France and Mars offers a one-way trip. Stare at the night. You'll see Mars hanging off the horn of the moon like a pendant. The dust on Mars is brown-red, no human in it. Everything looks silent and pure in a night sky on account of distance.

From Mars they will look down at us. Through a telescope we look tiny, through a microscope we look huge. In a human sky dust clouds mix with sparkles finely dispersed. The sun lights by day the moon at night. Let's sleep where there is no complaint. On the dark side of the moon one night lasts forever. On Mars everyone sleeps while I stay up late looking for the earth.

The Test

—for my daughter Anya

Yes or no questions on a brilliant white screen. Ten minutes to answer. What if no one listens? What if the sky you thought empty air were crumpled paper? What if loneliness were cured?

In the subjunctive skies be vast and may the earth hurtle through oceans of stars. In the imperative order me around: Do this, do that, clean your room, wipe your eyes. Who orders—the god of grammar? Destitute in the alley a toothless old man mutters illiteracies.

Gone mad with precision, the goddess of mathematics operates a glass tower with sharp corners. Everyone sees what no one touches. "God B" knows tubules of sperm and milk. You haven't begun to answer while others walk out smug. Your life baited on a question hook. But when you left your seat unanswered you felt a strange peace. You walked to the "iron door marked Emergency" and looked to the crumpled sky. Painted today in an irrealist mood, a regal blue. Black words leave a white screen for your brain: nothing but appearances or less apparent than dots of pepper.

"Come here," the Beloved says "and take my hand. You have passed every test, for I am not apparent at all."

Body And Soul

Ever wonder if all reactions wind up in the same sky? Could be elegance thrives there with petulance until a storm drops them both mixing heat and lightning fire and ice. When words come back to you will it look like a storm?

It rained all hours yesterday. This boat we're on is sinking, someone said. S.S. New Orleans. SOS New Orleans. But I heard a man singing on his bicycle "Body and Soul" and someone showered a wallet of green into the sidewalk saxophone case just before the torrent and in both cases that someone was me. I'm afraid that's the only way I know things happen around here: because there's a me. And especially because there's a you.

The Secret Child

The embryo is full of music. Nerves thread through the flesh. Sweet as cake with the sweetness of hope unborn. About the size of an olive to begin with—no, of a raisin or lemon seed —no, the size of a wisp a gist. The exact size of *no* budding *yes*. From the deep well of all wishing I have been born again, love says, just like tomorrow. And as sure as yesterday, love sings, I will be born again.

The Release of Vows

—for the chanting of Kol Nidre

On the evening of the Day of Atonement bats flew up from under the bridge in a black high-pitched cloud. The profane river reflected dimly a grey sky. It was calm inside her being She'd peeled away every thin darkness—the remaining light fled like a bird. A dove hovered in the bell tower, reappeared in the magician's palm. The cantor confessed her unworthiness and held the mournful congregation in her throat. The music recorded the flight of the bats' phantom applause. God disappeared with evening, drawing a line in the dark with black holes. At the event horizon the magician blessed the crowd—a dove flew from his mouth. The war of black and white goes on the war of male and female of day and night. The blessed and the damned joined hands the bats wavered between them. Doves battled crows, the mockingbird sang an inhuman psalm. King David would have been glad to hear that praise deep in the unnamable. He would have been glad, would have blessed that avian music with fluttering hands.

The Lessons

The cantor sang without his throat. He bled prayer through his pores. This was the logic of the suicide crow that hurled herself into the patio glass headlong. All of nature's pain was in her broken wing: the struggle of rocks towards speech, the struggle of atoms towards rock.

I struggle for words for even the simplest things. The fizz in the fire. I sink my good hand into a burning heart and pull it back covered with paint. What I've internalized recirculates. I am at the beginning of nothing. The crow teaches me her alphabet. The sun burns one and zero into my eyes.

The Errors of Religion

Something happens, half fact and half imagined. People write it. The miraculous part adds a glamor. The human hero makes room for the trans-human. The imagination spreads pinks and violets of sunset, flight of crows and doves, hurry of bats, falling stars. The wounds hide in blood, become splendid. The torture was actual the death was real but the miracle requires the drowned must be saved the dying man brought to life. Miriam shakes her tambourine and god is at her fingertips. But we turned our eyes to Sinai and learned new laws. Some fact and much imagination richly mixed. It's literature but to the reader it's history that hardens into dogma. The red paint dries. The light becomes the business plan of a priest. We are condemned to worn versions.

Azimuth

Horizons cross horizons. First steps baby steps black steps. The elevator door opens and the allergic child wheezes. As if underwater his eyes grey. As if nothing gripped my lungs in an iron hand, I sit up with apnea. Sleep has left me. My breath has left me. A knife cuts through the horizon a zenith plunges to a nadir. August on high: the dog star shines uneven light. The sound of jagged breaths. What is one man's life, one woman's? What life is we must mean. I drown in loneliness. I drown in splendor. Drown me in kindness then. Drown me in love. The search for goddesses in the sky and the search for breath where horizons collide. Last gasps. Where the world enters its numb zodiac where the stars reckon us as diminished angles, as broken minutes.

The Illustrated Book of God

I opened *The Illustrated Book of God*. It was written all of gold letters. There was a fire on page one. The flames licked the page. I stopped reading with my eyes and read with my tongue. I tasted vermillion. I put my ear to the page and heard the lions roar. I heard the clouds. I touched the bleak thorns of the acacia. I marched on oceans my feet grew weary. I sank into the delicious black mud with bare feet and bare bottom. I opened the door to the stranger who lit candles in the sun. I walked on the moon. I knew strange love of every kind nothing was forbidden. "I knew what other men thought they knew." The father came to me and blessed my broken mind. He comforted the mother who had lost her child. He sang of the shepherd and the shape. My body disappeared and I walked into pages. The gold letters left imprints on my subtle body. I knew and knew the end and the beginning. I tasted the water of loving-kindness and drank a fill. The peacocks led me to the horizon. The elephants recited their bible. The lions returned and ate my heart. I died in the dark of my last page. The book went on still unopened still unknown its hand beyond knowing.

Rehearsals

My wife—said the solitary actor —does not understand my death. She sees it only from a personal point of view. He should have been grateful but looked for a mystery quotient —headlights in a rear view mirror, a round spaceship spinning towards red suns. He imagined a long procession and a solemn pause. One stick of grandeur. Much time on earth is oblique soliloquy while your dog dreams of lipstick on her black smile. She has come to English after a million years of evolution —do you think she will waste a word on you now? The philosophical room in the house is the bathroom. The dog watches your wife moue in the mirror. We are all rehearsing—it's just that some of us get better lines. Where has her sweet lipstick gotten to—the coral in the gold vial?

A Block of No

A big block of no—might have been radium for the look of it. Sat for a while sucking light around it softly. A thin margin of darkness like a reverse atmosphere. The outer crust was still warm and who knew the trouble of the core? I slunk off afraid thinking ignoring was a better plan. That has always been my plan — along with dimming. But not twenty steps away felt a stone in my shoe. Then I knew this one was bad. My sock soaked in blood which I pretended was a choice in scarlet when I saw others struggling—a whole line of them on a city street. Some scratched their scalps at the hairline. A few had hands down their pants. Poor Bastards! I shouted. Idiots! *Idiots savants*! But they spoke their own language lost in complications. Their rhythmic scratching made music in my chest only an insect would call melody. A nymph eleven years in a dirt crypt took wing with a myriad. You call that a life cycle? I limped on. Now a pebble in my ear blocked the sound of thought, or was that thought? A sharp hot pink broke my bronchia at each aitch. The burns' prod, a sting to shake my hips. I heard the whole orchestra: violins gonifs mangoes. Someone's always juggling mangoes when I'm in pain. Clowns! Gold diggers! An iron crust—but at the heart sweet flame.

The Poetry Pure

There are no words for you. Pre-existing condition awaiting skin, a hand reaching for the moon. To pluck an Adam's apple or "apple of the eye," Hebraism for "precious." There's no cure for normal. You swim towards Venus. By the time you come through the thunderstorm we passengers will have pulsed our bags. I saw lightning surround you as you plummeted up into a vagrant cloud. I can't possibly touch you. There's nothing serious in you yet I take you seriously. Your secret sauce: you are all flavor. Because you are empty you hold space. Inescapable, you are always escaping me.

Never Saw a Goddess Go

Some day you'll learn where you end and the world begins. Not every touch is gravity but you fall according to your own laws. Wherever you land it's for the first time, which makes you lovable. Your body has a mind of its own. You don't define you encroach but the feeling is mutual: the world comes closer thing by thing. Brick would hug your toe not stub, the walls kiss your silent arm to speech, the floor rise and fall with your breath and clouds envelop you. You make your own vault. It's not your fault the world rushes to meet you. The royal of you tips armchairs towards your thigh, bows an apple branch to brush your hair.

Luckily I bumped into you.

Asymptote

—for Zeno and Kafka

Me—the target of all my devotion, an arrow splintering into itself. Lost in trajectory collecting attention or dismay at every point of the curve. Ah, I am going up. Now I'm going down. Feeling flat. Stalled. Ego Zeno, most terrifying zero. Was I never moving? Is all motion a joke? Time nearly catches me but never touches. I turn to see terror on Achilles' face, his arms pumping, his heart upside down. The shell I've grown around me is thick with brittle edges. I barely move. Yet I call it home.

Yogi

—h/t Mark Zanger

"Yogi Berra was a great bad ball hitter. Even if he had to golf or tomahawk, he was clutch." The balls I hit are all bad: that's why I hit them. That's where anger turns into beauty. They say there are no bad dogs but *they* are mostly dog trainers in their pride. Pride and shame are two ends of the same bat. Shame makes every bad ball your fault. That's where Yogi comes in, the best Yankee philosopher since Emerson, the Buddha squatting behind every batter. He observes the violence of the perfect pitch, the smack in the deep pocket of his fat glove. Thanks to Yogi there are no bad restaurants, no bad decisions, no bad balls. "When you come to a fork in the road, take it." Maybe a scratch single, a dribbler to the left, a ball just out of reach of a diving glove, Yogi motoring to first. He came back as a huge gentle black dog who takes the bite out of every bark. Soon all the neighbor dogs are following Yogi to the restaurant no one goes to anymore.

Brooding

I am sitting on an egg. If it doesn't hatch it will explode. Perhaps *explode* is too harsh. The egg will merely shatter. I too will merely shatter. *Merely* doesn't matter. I am inside the egg looking through the shell and the world looks vague. Someone has scumbled it with words. The words are all white. I need black in my world if I'm going to read the wrong names. Red lies beside me here in the yolk. A little spot that feels mammalian. When I hatch I will be dying but what do I know of dying? I am all about hatching. I'm a hatchling-in-waiting.

The Invention of the Hurricane

—for Leigh Randolph

In a corner of hell where they keep busy sewing clouds someone had an idea. They practiced chasing each other in rounds then taught a fog to chase its tail. Soon giants brushed into motion whistling and humming and shaking their fat hips. They wore lightning hats and drizzly blue rain jackets. The inventors tossed ice cubes and violence onto their heads and sent them on their way to the coast of Africa in a school bus. The giants danced off the bus spinning and singing and whipping while a dream kept reminding them of winter weather. Better hurry then. Most of their fury danced in a circle so it took an outside wind to bump them west. The Leeward Islands leaned together. No one could forecast where the dance would end. With a drunken belch they fell out screaming gathering heat at their feet from a tub of wrath. A whole summer of sun shot into their shock. They wrapped hot moist air around them like wool sweaters. The heat made them dizzy, which spun them faster. Then they all came together in an eye that couldn't see. But Cuba loomed and the green tongue of Florida.

Butter Moon

At a hint of punishment his fingers retracted like petals. With any ambition, he would have been a rose. As a full moon he sat in his own hot sky melting. Actually people were complaining about the moon. A few boycotted. They averted their gazes and walked slowly as if in awe of their own feet. Whatever pilgrim thought ventured his way he welcomed with open ear. Which led him to this strange way of rising to occasion bumping his head against the back of the tomb. Forgetting is low-grade nirvana. What's forgotten best lasts best like a grave no one visits. The dead joke, *we are less forgiving*. But to stand beneath the sun bending in all directions as it treks across the sky? That would be one pilgrim too many. If you pull him up by the roots he'll fly. Or want to.

Waiting for Landfall

—for my friends in New Orleans

A sweetness in the mind stands ready to be evicted. Sometimes all it takes is the right knock on the door or you can cruise in with full power at 400 knots and drag ocean behind you. Now that would be a storm to scar the heart. I'll look up the record but it seems to be gold. A skull washed in a pond, the measure of innocence in a bone. We drown and clown. You can catalog your complaints if you want but a gigantic wave'll scatter all your toothpicks. Believe me everyone's got a handful and you may need both for the weather. Drop everything and drive from danger. It's all washing through you: blood, electricity. There are colors coming out of your eyes.

Can You Ever Love?

Can you ever love what isn't you? There's an intelligence angle but throwing the data away clears the screen. That way facing this way facing that way I can see my face in the mirror isn't yours. It's the back of my head looking cross-eyed. The words you say aren't my words. Yet somehow I want to listen. They *falleth* like the dew. And when they do they *doeth*. You do for me more than due. Sometimes I fall asleep in my own cloud and when the sun breaks through the grass is moist and the worms are happy. I open my eyes and there is you.

Dragonfly

—for my mother

Animals eat here. Some so tiny their world is but a
stone. Hunger a pinpoint, they drink a dew. The garden
throbs with them. Iridium, bits of rainbow, needle
greens, penetrating blues. Who named them *darning
needles—nightmare horses,* names born of fear?
Their veined wings—a double set—beat back the air
of occasion, become occasion. They keep distance
from nectar: they snatch mosquitoes, tear their wings
in the air. Their head all eyes. *How could an insect,
a dog have life and not you?* They snatch elegy, mid-
flight—hover with glints of loss. Unlike dragonflies,
memory stings. The adventure of who you were lives
in me. And when I go who will carry this envelope?
Who read the letter inside?

Magnetic Resonance

—for the nurse Angel

So in a situation like this you want to lay still. Not step on a slippery horizon. All beyond is blue space a blue that blackens: simple words will do whole words. There are word fractions even imaginary words the square root of minus one is *i*. A fractionated ego is volatile. Gases leak all over. I describe a world that can't find the square root of minus me. We'll have to make it up then it fits quite nicely into a number of equations. Someone will be figuring absolute me. I sit quietly unbuttoned. It's a room for waiting. How tie my own gown from behind? I need help the machine resonates but not musically and the bouncing jolts. The nurse Angel handed me earphones but my choices were talk radio light rock or country. I made the least bad choice as usual. The unsolved equations pile up on the horizon. A line of zeroes there goes far out into space. Some of those numbers have my name on them. The square root of zero is zero but you can't divide anything by it. The infinite yawns from boredom. It's not only inconsiderable it can't be counted on at all. It has no personality. Inside the throbbing machine I am counting on one I even seem to know by name. If *i* is entirely imaginary, why can't you be imagined too?

Incident on Memory Lane

—for my mother

So like twilight to show up just when you need it.
There are no rules any more that's one of the rules.
If I could just hold my breath: no one else to hold it.
In principle we will all be forgotten where so-and-
so meets on and on. You might prefer anonymity
but a gas station's ahead and baby needs to take a
break. Take it then. Are you taking something for
disappointment? I missed seeing you yesterday and
all the days, mother. They say I have your eyes and
yet I can't see you anymore. They say the baby has
your face.

Boners

Not knowing what they are where they come from what they are for, an infant boy. Innocent ignorant just this then that. Free of purpose. What is firm what is soft what takes over what makes a point out of no desire but to be itself. Comes and goes rises falls an impromptu an improv a knocking at the door what new guest arrives a headlong spirit of blood urging towards parts unknown. Then later a big joke in the giggling classroom and a strange pride a secret ingredient an impulse but still mostly a premonition. The afterthought like a quiet moment curling into itself as if defeat were also whispering in the midst of life as if death were also calling faintly from distance your name.

Acknowledgments:

Big thanks to Noah Warren and to Laura Mullen, Bill Lavender, Hank Lazer, Richard Katrovas, Jonathan Penton, Jessica Faust for their kind attention.

Several of these poems appeared in *Beyond the Margins*, *Bosque*, *Forward*, *Image*, *New Orleans Review*, *Southern Review*, *Unlikely Stories*, *Xavier Review*. The author is grateful to the editors.

"In Praise of the Ladder" in *Image #98*

"I Traveled Through A Land Of Men" in *Image #100*

"Yogi", "The Living Hive" in *Southern Review* Summer 2018.

"The Remedy for the Remedy", "Satisfaction", *Across the Margin*, November 29, 2017 http://acrossthemargin.com/two-poems-rodger-kamenetz/

"Boners", "The Brewery of the Arts", "A Dialogue of Yous" *New Orleans Review* July 2017 http://www.neworleansreview.org/a-dialogue-of-yous/

"In Loneliness", "Where the Man Sat" "Palindromes to Harass Sarah Palin" *Unlikely Stories Mark V* June 2017 http://www.unlikelystories.org/content/in-loneliness-where-the-man-sat-and-palindromes-to-harass-sarah-palin

"Dream Recovery Project", "The War Shop", *Bosque* 5 (2015)

"Autobiography of a Flower", "Words for a Dying Man", "What About the Father","The Last Word" *Xavier Review*, 37:2 (2017) pp. 112-115

"What is Hamlet's Father's Name", "An Invention of Time", *Bosque* 7, November 2017.

"The Necessary Killings", *Forward*, July 18, 2014

"For Emily Brontë", *Unlikely Stories*, June 2018

"If It Were My Dream 4", *Live Mag #15*

Notes

The Necessary Killings July 18, 2014. "The United Nations Security Council calls for an immediate ceasefire but neither Israel nor Hamas agrees. (*Washington Post*)"

The Gold Statue On May 16, 2017 Confederate General P.T. Beauregard and the horse he rode in on were taken off their pedestal in front of the New Orleans Museum of Art.

Christian Families Translation of "*Familles Chrétiennes*", *Derniers poèmes* Paris: Gallimard, 1961. p.123

The Safe Orbit "*eppur si muove*"-- "and yet it moves", supposedly muttered by Galileo as he foreswore his "heresy" of heliocentrism.

Love Your Neighbor Translation of "*Amour du Prochain*", *Derniers poèmes* Paris: Gallimard, 1961. p.151. The French Jewish Catholic prose poet Max Jacob wore "*l'étoile jaune*" and was later arrested by the Gestapo. He died at the internment camp at Drancy.

Pocket Dial Sri Ramana Maharshi was a self-taught teacher of experiential Advaita. His great text is "Who Am I?" an inquiry into self-realization.

Prospectus for Yonder The Hebrew letter "aleph" is the number one. In Cantor's mathematics it is infinity. Blake "Auguries of Innocence" "To see a World in a Grain of Sand/ And a Heaven in a Wild Flower/ Hold Infinity in the palm of your hand/ And Eternity in an hour"

For Emily Brontë A review of Jeffrey Wright's sonnet sequence *Triple Crown* whose muse is Emily Brontë. Sarah Vaughn and Allen Ginsberg are tutelary deities of Newark. Elvis served as a teenage "shabbes goy" in Memphis. Ellis Bell is the pen name under which Brontë published *Wuthering Heights*.

Verlan A *verlan* is French language anagram slang, for instance *fuij* for *juif*. Used pejoratively.

The Brewery of the Arts "Time absorbed me like a stone", said Herbert Kearney a New Orleans based visual artist; the fantastic "experiments" are actual.

On The Path of Totality August 21, 2017 a total eclipse of the sun in large swaths of North America.

Talking Dirty to Siri All quotes in italics are from Siri.

Forbidden Words The Hebrew word "*chashmal*" (Ezekiel 1:4) is usually translated "electrum" but no one really knows what it means. Rabbis restricted young people from reading Ezekiel and the legend of the boy who violated that restriction is told here. "The appearance of a likeness of a man." Ezekiel 1:26.

Poetry Itself "a raid on the inarticulate" T.S. Eliot, "East Coker."

Another Good Day "evening morning one day" Genesis 1:5. The Hebrew day begins at sunset.

The Test *The Test: Why Our Schools are Obsessed with Standardized Testing But You Don't Have to Be* by Anya Kamenetz. "God B(iology)" from James Merrill. "...iron door" from "Questions and Answers" by Yehuda Amichai.

The Release of Vows *kol nidre* or "all vows" is an Aramaic text sung solemnly on the eve of Yom Kippur.

The Errors of Religion We can speak of two revelations, one at Sinai and one at the Red Sea. "god at fingertips" Per Rashi on Exodus 15:2 "they pointed to Him with the finger: a maidservant at the Sea saw that which prophets did not see."

Azimuth is the apparent horizontal direction of a star, zenith the imaginary point directly above where you stand on earth, nadir the same below.

The Illustrated Book of God "subtle body" aka "the light body" "the rainbow body", "the body of bliss". To me it is the dream body. "I knew what other men..." Rimbaud, "The Drunken Boat."

The Poetry Pure Or "*la poésie pure*"-- Poetry approaching the conditions of music. "apple of the eye" is a Hebraism, a mistranslation now idiomatic in English. The original meaning was "pupil of the eye."

Never Saw A Goddess Go Sonnet 130.

Asymptote In geometry a line that approaches a curve but never attains it. In Zeno's paradoxes-- an arrow cannot move, Achilles will never catch up to a tortoise. Or Kafka's parables of futility such as "A Message from the Emperor".

Yogi The opening quote is from author Mark Zanger. The second quote is attributed to Yogi Berra.

The Invention of the Hurricane Written for a friend in Florida awaiting Hurricane Irma, September 2017.

Magnetic Resonance In mathematics the square root of minus one -- or i-- is an 'imaginary" number that turns out to be necessary in a number of crucial real-world equations.

.

Lavender Ink
lavenderink.org

CPSIA information can be obtained
at www.ICGtesting.com
Printed in the USA
FFHW020414010419
51357054-56829FF